IMAGES
of America
MERRILL

Known as bird's-eye views, panoramas, or perspective maps, these detailed illustrations were very popular with residents of growing communities during the latter half of the 19th century. Because people expected their city to be depicted as prosperous, the artist added details like smoke streaming from factory chimneys. In 1880, Jenny and the surrounding area had a population of just over 2,000. By 1883, Jenny, renamed Merrill, had a population of 7,000. (Courtesy of Library of Congress, Geography and Map Division.)

ON THE COVER: A group enjoys an outing on the Prairie River in Stange Public Park around 1910. The three-arch bridge seen in the background was built in 1904 by Fred Hesterman. It took him a year of hauling stone before he could begin construction. The bridge was placed in the National Register of Historic Places in 1998. (Courtesy of Merrill Historical Society.)

IMAGES
of America
MERRILL

Robin L. Comeau in cooperation
with the T.B. Scott Free Library
and Merrill Historical Society, Inc.

Copyright © 2013 by Robin L. Comeau in cooperation with the T.B. Scott Free Library and
   Merrill Historical Society, Inc.
ISBN 978-1-5316-6121-2

Published by Arcadia Publishing
Charleston, South Carolina

Library of Congress Control Number: 2012949291

For all general information, please contact Arcadia Publishing:
Telephone 843-853-2070
Fax 843-853-0044
E-mail sales@arcadiapublishing.com
For customer service and orders:
Toll-Free 1-888-313-2665

Visit us on the Internet at www.arcadiapublishing.com

To the citizens of Merrill

Contents

Acknowledgements		6
Introduction		7
1.	Jenny Bull Falls to Merrill	9
2.	The Railroad	11
3.	Logging and Farming	19
4.	Around the Town	29
5.	City of Parks	59
6.	Sports and Leisure	73
7.	Reading, Writing, and Religion	85
8.	Seven Wonders of Merrill	95
9.	The Fair	107
10.	Mother Nature	119

Acknowledgments

This production would not have been possible without the superb photographic collections of the T.B. Scott Free Library (TBSFL) and the Merrill Historical Society (MHS). I gratefully acknowledge the following individuals for their expertise with this project: Don Litzer, assistant director at the T.B. Scott Free Library; Bea Lebal, Pat Burg, and other members and staff of the Merrill Historical Society; Dan Wendorf, City of Merrill Parks and Recreation Department director (COM); and Deborah Moellendorf of the Lincoln County UW-Extension office (LCUWX). I would like to especially thank Beverly King of the Merrill Historical Society for her invaluable editing assistance and guidance in choosing photographs. Thank you to a special friend, Ruth Pope Dreger, for sharing photographs of her family's dairy and recollections of her many years as an educator. Special thanks to my Arcadia Publishing editors Winnie Timmons and Katie Toussaint for their guidance and expertise. I extend a heartfelt thank you to my family and friends for their encouragement, love, and support.

INTRODUCTION

A look back at Merrill's early days—the landscape, activities, and businesses—connects today's citizens with those of the past. Merrill was originally a logging town established as a village referred to as Jenny Bull Falls or simply Jenny. Divided by the Wisconsin and Prairie Rivers, it was first inhabited by the Ojibwe/Chippewa Native Americans, and by 1843 a trading post was constructed near the village. Drawn to the big pine forests, it was Pete Kelley who first began to log the pinery. He sent for O.B. Smith and a group of others to join him to do the work. They arrived in 1844, just four years before Wisconsin reached statehood. Smith was also responsible for opening up roads both north and south of the area between 1854 and 1860. Andrew Warren, joining the crowd about a year later, constructed a dam across the Wisconsin River that was completed in 1849; this would eventually power his sawmill along with others. In 1851, the first fleet of lumber left Jenny, floating down the Wisconsin River for Illinois. John and Alexander Stewart came in as the first big lumber operators and logged all over the area from 1852 to 1872. To support the lumber commerce, citizens of Jenny soon added additional boardinghouses, mercantile and blacksmith shops, and liveries. At the first meeting of the county board held on October 24, 1874, Jenny was designated as the seat for Lincoln County government. The first courthouse was built in 1881. Daniel Scott began running a daily stage between Wausau and Jenny in 1875, with July 1 marking the first day of mail service. Churches, schools, fire departments, and banks soon followed.

Early promises of a railway system in the 1850s and 1860s finally reaching Jenny had investors mortgaging farms and land. Half of the community was left badly in debt after the railroad schemes went bust. It is no wonder that citizens viewed the arrival of the railroad in 1880 as a blessing of better things to come. Even the town's name of Jenny was formally changed to Merrill in honor of the arriving railroad's general manager, Sherburn S. Merrill. With the coming of the railroad, there was a scramble for business locations, and in a very short time the population of Merrill exploded. The East Side, West Side, and Sixth Ward—all locations for mills and businesses—were joined together by bridges and incorporated as a city in 1883. The first city council met and named Thomas B. Scott as Merrill's first mayor.

The peak of the lumbering boom came in 1892, and by 1900, with the timber industry tapering off, the community was compelled to diversify its economy. The forests had been skinned of pines, so the lumbering men began to concentrate on hardwoods. At one time, nearly 20 mills in the area produced hardwood lumber. Merrill's present recognition as a principal millwork center seems only natural in light of the lumbering background of the community. In addition, the fertile soils in the area have continued to serve agricultural interests well. Although the number of farms has declined over the years, the agriculture industry remains one of Lincoln County's most profitable.

Merrill, as it is known today, was largely built between 1883 and 1903: a new courthouse was built in 1903, a steel bridge came in 1892, the business district took shape, civic buildings were constructed, park areas were established and landscaped, and the population quickly rose to 7,000. The T.B. Scott Free Library was established in 1891 in part with $10,000 left by Scott in his will, and in 1911, with funding from Andrew Carnegie, a new library building was completed. It was placed in the National Register of Historic Places in 1974. The first telephone office was built by the Wisconsin Telephone Company in 1881 with a total of 20 telephones. By 1896, a local phone exchange was organized and continued to operate until 1910, when it was again reorganized. The Merrill Electric Railway and Lighting Company was formed in 1889 and, in 1890, built a street railway system. The cars in this system featured a single wheel at the end of a pole running under a copper wire hung down the middle of the street. This type of installation was the first of its kind in the state of Wisconsin. A trackless trolley system was introduced in 1913, the first of its kind in the country. This system was a desirable solution to transportation problems in outlying areas of the city where laying track would have been expensive. The entire system was replaced in favor of buses in November 1921 due to rising maintenance costs and falling revenue.

Recreation for a growing industrial and urban nation attracted many from the larger cities north for relaxation. Some of the natural areas containing streams, as well as brush and trees not profitable to harvest, were suitable for something else: recreation. Early on, boys' and girls' camps and eventually scouting camps offered wilderness and pioneer experiences. As the camping craze spread, the Wisconsin State Board of Forestry was also formulating plans for forest reserves. The state purchased areas of land that remained protected, unable to be developed agriculturally. It was hopeful these tracks of land would bring tourists, campers, hunters, fishermen, and revenue into the area. One such area, Council Grounds State Park, was given to the state by the City of Merrill in 1938. Prior to being classified as a state park in 1974, the area was called Council Grounds State Forest and at one time Roadside Park. Surrounded by acres of natural resources, Merrill continues to develop areas for mixed recreational uses, attracting tourists to the area for four seasons of fun.

The heritage and history of Merrill will soon be showcased in a new history and culture center. The Merrill Historical Society broke ground on the construction project in 2012. The center will hold a library for history and genealogical research, provide space for community events, and create a modern museum to make Merrill history accessible to the community. Through advocacy, education, and publication of the history of the community, the society seeks to preserve a "sense of place." Merrill has 25 buildings in the National Register of Historic Places, including the Center Avenue Historic District with 20 heritage homes built from 1885 to the 1930s.

Today, with a population of just under 10,000, Merrill has a regional economy that remains highly diversified and a spirited community with a great vision for the future while keeping an eye on the past.

One
Jenny Bull Falls to Merrill

Word spread among early settlements in the southern part of the Wisconsin Territory of opportunities up north in the pinery. There were reports of immense stands of pine forests in a wild region at the junction of the Wisconsin and Prairie Rivers. This area was first known as Jenny Bull Falls, then Jenny Falls, and finally Jenny. Although first inhabited by members of the Ojibwe/Chippewa tribe, by 1843 a trading post had already been established. A year later, O.B. Smith and a group of men made their way on foot from Chicago to see for themselves. The logging boom was on!

Sawmills sprang up along the river, and dams were constructed to power the mills. While the convenience of the Wisconsin River afforded loggers a means to transport their goods, a railroad would make the trek quicker and easier, with the added bonus of carrying passengers; however, the problem was that the railway network was well south of the area. In the mid-1860s, Jenny citizens bought into various railroad schemes that went bust—dreams and pocketbooks were shattered. Jenny and its citizens would have to wait 20 more years before a railroad would become reality. Finally completed in 1880, the Wisconsin Valley Railroad extended its tracks from Wausau to Jenny. This connected Jenny with the massive Chicago, Milwaukee & St. Paul Railroad system. In 1881, the village board formally changed the name of the city from Jenny to Merrill in honor of the railroad company's general manager, Sherburn S. Merrill.

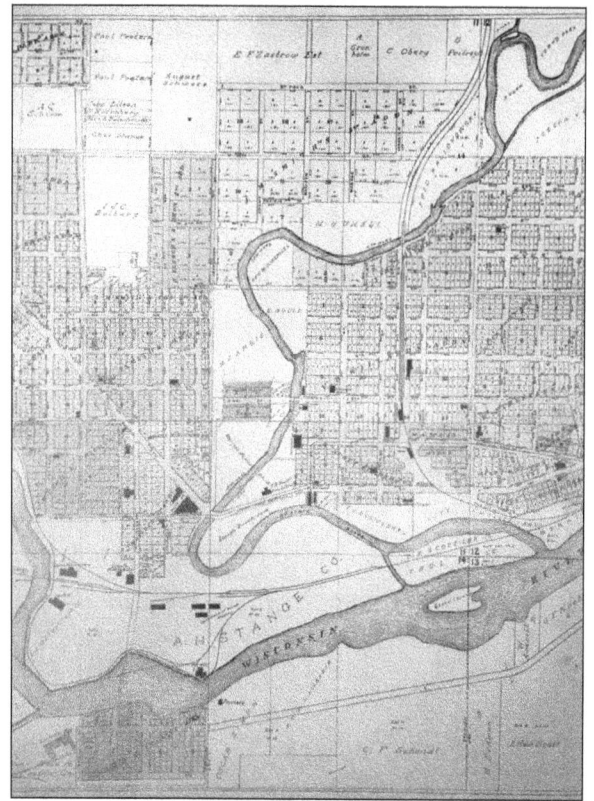

Merrill city planners took full advantage of the location started by the settlers of Jenny by laying out a system of streets, bridges, and dams that would serve the city well into the future as depicted in the 1914 plat map of a portion of the city (left). Merrill's namesake, Sherburn S. Merrill, was born in New Hampshire in 1818 and left home at the age of 16 (below). Upon settling in Milwaukee, he found a job in the rail yard and eventually worked his way up to foreman. In 1865, he became general manager of the Chicago, Milwaukee, & St. Paul Railroad and quickly became one of the best-known railroad men in the country. He died in Milwaukee in 1885. None of his descendants were ever known to have lived in Merrill. (At left, courtesy of MHS; below, Milwaukee County Historical Society.)

Two
THE RAILROAD

Prior to the advent of rails, transportation was conducted primarily by following rudimentary paths that had been used by the Native Americans and widened by early settlers to accommodate a stagecoach or wagon. The Wisconsin and Prairie Rivers offered a means for logs to get from one place to another, but only for the soft pinewood that would float and only during the months that the waterways were open.

With the arrival of the railroad in the spring of 1881 came the dreams of prosperity for the settlers of Merrill. Improving transportation meant that goods and services could be moved into and out of the area with increased efficiency. Passenger cars offered a comfortable way to travel for individuals doing business in other towns and also satisfied the curiosity of those wishing to see what Merrill had to offer. In just two short years, following the arrival of the railroad to Merrill, the population had grown from 2,000 to 7,000; the construction of business and residential buildings increased three-fold in just one year. Train depots were built to accommodate passengers and the arrival and departure of goods. Depots also housed other business ventures, such as telegram and telegraph services, and were popular gathering places for townsfolk to celebrate the arrival of a train.

With the introduction of the automobile and improvements in the highway systems, the railroad soon fell out of favor as the first choice for travel, as freight could now be shipped from one place to another quicker and more efficiently. While passenger service to and from Merrill was eliminated in the mid-1950s, the romance of the railroad and the importance and promise it brought to the area continues to endure today.

This section of track connected the village of Jenny to the city of Wausau, located just to the south. After the railway system arrived, the area economy prospered. Additional businesses were established to meet the needs of settlers and visitors. Trains offered a means to transport and receive goods year-round. Below, an 1882 railroad and postal map shows the completed railway line to the city of Merrill. In 1887, additional track was laid north of the city to connect Merrill with the newly formed city of Tomahawk. (Above, courtesy of MHS; below, Library of Congress, Geography and Map Division.)

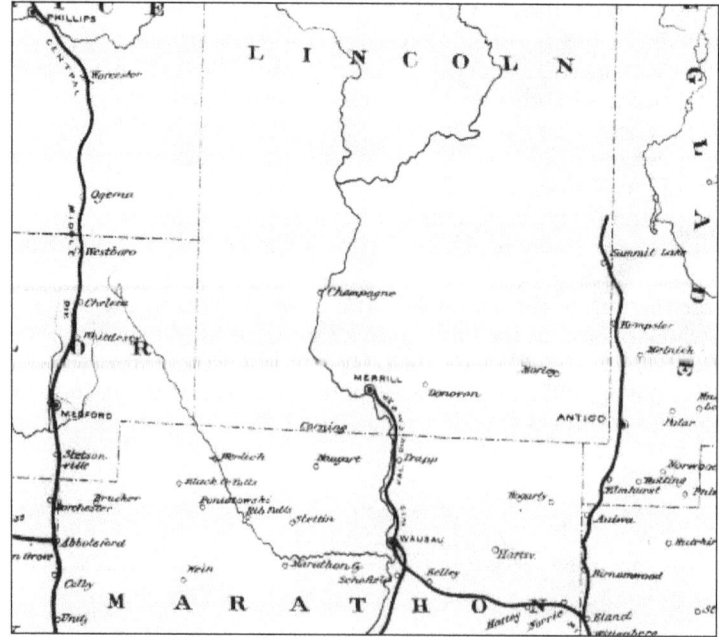

Stange Lumber Company's two-truck shay, Engine No. 3, leads a string of Chicago, Milwaukee & St. Paul flat rail cars being loaded by the company's Decker log loader in the early to mid 1900s. The Stange Lumber Company was started in 1895 by August H. Stange. (Courtesy of TBSFL.)

The Chicago, Milwaukee & St. Paul Railroad passenger train roars through Merrill in the early 1900s. Railroads increased the efficiency of transporting lumber, as well as offering an alternative means of travel for individuals. Trains would continue to carry passengers into and out of Merrill well into the 1950s. (Courtesy of MHS.)

Flatcars stacked with logs sit ready for pickup at the August H. Stange lumber mill in Merrill. Stange built a lumber enterprise with saw and planing mills in Eagle River, Wisconsin, and LaGrande Oregon. (Courtesy of TBSFL.)

Employees of the Chicago, Milwaukee & St. Paul Railroad pose at the Merrill depot in the early 1890s. The advent of the railroad brought a variety of much needed employment opportunities, both at the depot and on the railway line. (Courtesy of MHS.)

A late-1920s Shay No. 5 locomotive, belonging to the Kinzel Lumber Company, stops on the track with a load of logs. Below, a Milwaukee Road flatcar is loaded with pulpwood by workers of the Kinzel Lumber Company in the New Wood area, situated west of Merrill. The Kinzel Lumber Company (formerly the H.W. Wright Company), organized in 1914 by August H. Stange, was one of the largest timber and sawmill operations in the region. Stange, who came to Merrill in 1881, owned the Stange Lumber Company nearby. It was said to be the largest sash and door company in the country. (Both courtesy of MHS.)

Chicago, Milwaukee, St. Paul & Pacific Railroad section crew at Merrill is pictured above in the 1950s. From left to right are Fred Zimmerman, Arthur Freiberg, William Frazier, Richard "Peck" Cherwenka, Eric King, Martin Johnson, Henry Litke, Ed Mittlesteadt, Matthew Huven, and Charles Strassman. Section crews or section gangs, as they were commonly known, were responsible for maintaining a several miles–long section of track. They were responsible for replacing rotted ties, tamping loose spikes, tightening bolts, reinforcing roadbeds, and clearing weeds and debris. Below, a Chicago, Milwaukee & St. Paul section crew uses a handcar in the late 1890s. (Both courtesy of MHS.)

The Chicago, Milwaukee, St. Paul & Pacific Railroad's section crew in Merrill carries a rail to place on new ties near the Weinbrenner Shoe Company building about 1949. While passenger train service began to wane in the area during the 1950s, industries relied heavily on rail to transport goods. (Courtesy of MHS.)

An employee of the Chicago, Milwaukee & St. Paul Railroad straddles a velocipede in the rail yard in Merrill. The three-wheeled vehicle, popular during the 1880s, was primarily used by railway officials to inspect track sections. Weighing about 140 pounds, it was light enough for one man to lift off the tracks or to turn around. (Courtesy of MHS.)

Marie Henson and her children—from left to right, Christine, Kathleen, and John—prepare to board a Chicago, Milwaukee & St. Paul train at Merrill for a ride to Tomahawk in 1949. That same year, area newspapers advertised "Harvest Excursions" run by rail to "all prominent land points in Northern Iowa, Western Minnesota, Dakota and Nebraska, at one fare for the round trip." (Courtesy of MHS.)

A passenger train arrives at the Merrill depot in the early years of the 20th century. This passenger depot was operational from the late 1890s to the early 1950s. Another service located here was the Railway Express Agency. In later years, the building served as a youth center called the Depot before being demolished in 1976. (Courtesy of TBSFL.)

Three
LOGGING AND FARMING

Just as pine forests beckoned to lumberjacks, the promise of abundant land encouraged an influx of immigrant farmers anxious to stake a claim. In the early 1800s, public land could be purchased for $1.25 an acre through a land patent. The Homestead Act of 1862 allowed the public to settle up to 160 acres of public land if they lived on it for five years and grew crops or made improvements. The land under this act did not cost anything other than the filing fee.

As the logging boom of the late 1800s began to wane, some lumberjacks moved on, and the cutover land, complete with stumps, was there for the taking. Even land that had yet to be cleared offered homesteaders ample lumber for buildings and fences. It was not easy work, but the end rewards and dreams of a nice farm and comfortable living was more than enough for some. In time, traditional logging gave way to other manufacturing interests, such as sash and bind, woodenware pails, toothpicks, windows, and doors. The ability of residents to diversify manufacturing as supplies of big pine dwindled speaks to the creativity and perseverance of a proud people. Today, forests cover 70 percent of Lincoln County, and farmers own and manage 15 percent of the county's land.

While there are three percent fewer dairy farms than a decade ago, dairy farming is still the county's leading agricultural business. Just as the harvesting of trees sustained settlers, the planting and harvesting of Christmas trees pumps thousands of dollars back into the local economy today. And so it is that timber and farming coexist and, just like in the past, continue to play an important role in the future of the Merrill area.

A crew relaxes after laying ties for logging railroad tracks in the early 1900s. The ties were freshly cut from the right-of-way and were commonly referred to as axe ties as they were hewn by hand, usually with a broad axe. (Courtesy of TBSFL.)

Members of a logging crew, along with an unidentified woman who likely delivered lunch, pause with their team and load in the late 1800s. Logs of this size were common during the logging boom of the 1800s. (Courtesy of TBSFL.)

A camp such as the one seen above, belonging to the Kinzel Lumber Company, was commonplace during the early to mid-1900s and became the home of many through the long winter months. Below, the kitchen crew waits for loggers in the camp cookhouse. Since the workday was often 10 hours long, it was not uncommon for cooks to prepare three meals. Typical meals included boiled meat, potatoes, hash, biscuits, pancakes, baked beans, and coffee. Most lumber camp cooks were men, but occasionally women were employed. (Above, courtesy of MHS; below, TBSFL.)

A group of unidentified lumberjacks poses with its team in the early 1900s. Logs were pulled out of the woods in the winter, piled by the river, and when ice thawed in the spring were floated downstream to the mills. (Courtesy of TBSFL.)

Trucks added a different kind of horsepower to haul a load of logs this size. Logging roads in the mid-1900s were at times nothing more than wide foot trails, and traditional horsepower was still used to navigate into and out of the woods. (Courtesy of TBSFL.)

Logging camp construction of this type was common in Wisconsin in the 1880s. A separate shanty was used for the bunkhouse, camp cookhouse, stable, and storage. Logging crews moved into the camps around mid-November and usually stayed until the spring thaw. (Courtesy of TBSFL.)

Logging in the early 1900s was managed with hand tools such as cant hooks, two-man saws, and an ax. The work was hard but offered a fair and steady wage. Oxen and/or horses were used to pull or skid out the wood. A staged photograph such as this was often made into a postcard. (Courtesy of TBSFL.)

In the early 1900s, the logging boom was waning. After most of the pines had been harvested, the land was essentially left clear cut. Skidding timber was made a little easier with the introduction of steam-powered crawlers. (Courtesy of TBSFL.)

A typical logging crew poses with tools of the trade in the late 1800s. The men and boys who worked in the woods were often individuals who came and went with the seasons, earning enough money in the winter to help sustain their farms through summer. (Courtesy of TBSFL.)

A steam tractor is shown above as part of a typical farming operation in the early 1900s. Working alongside the other kind of horsepower, improvements in farm machinery, as well as tractors, increased the efficiency and lessened the workload. Below, an unidentified farmer works the field with traditional horsepower in the mid-1800s. (Above, courtesy of TBSFL; below, author's collection.)

At left, an unidentified farmhand forks hay from a single-cylinder hay loader. The loader was attached to the back of a wagon and picked loose hay off of the ground. This hay-making equipment was typical for farm operations in the 1920s and 1930s. Below, a farm crew uses a horse-drawn hay baler and binders to put up hay in the 1800s. (At left, courtesy of MHS; below, TBSFL.)

One dairy that served the Merrill area for 55 years was founded by Benjamin Pope in the early 1900s and known over its existence as East Side Dairy, Cream Top Dairy, and Pope Dairy. The dairy was located on the Pope family farm, about one mile north of Merrill on what is now known as County Road K. Above, barn boss Hans Hauptmann poses with the dairy wagon used to deliver milk in the early 1900s. Below, Cora Will, daughter of Harold Pope, stands on the running board of a 1929 Model A Ford delivery truck. (Both courtesy of Ruth Pope Dreger.)

Dairy farming is the major agricultural industry in Lincoln County. In 2011, the county had 575 farms with an average size of 151 acres. Seen above is an aerial view of Dreger Brothers farm in May 1964. Pictured below is Dreger Brothers herd of black and white Holsteins, the most popular milk cows in Wisconsin. Their popularity stems from the fact that they have the ability to produce more milk than any other breed. (Both courtesy of Ruth Pope Dreger.)

Four
AROUND THE TOWN

The business district of Merrill is naturally divided into east and west by the Prairie River. Main Street makes the same division at the point it crosses the river. At the time of the first settlers, around 1847, the primary business interest was lumbering. The fact that the location of the mills followed the natural advantage of the river has resulted in the elongated, geographical outline of the present city. Shortly after the establishment of Lincoln County in 1874, resolutions passed establishing the county seat in the area commonly known as Jenny. At the time of incorporation in 1883, the city's primary businesses supported the logging industry, sawmills, boardinghouses, blacksmiths, and liveries. City government buildings, a courthouse, jail, fire departments, waterworks, banks, schools, and churches added to the infrastructure.

To support the growing population of Merrill, which hit 7,000 by 1895, grocery, hardware, department, and furniture stores, meat markets, and a hospital were added to the business complex. With the depletion of the supply of pine timber, which was formerly the basis of Merrill's industrial life, a wide diversity of manufacturing enterprises sprang up, and everything from machinery, canned goods, knitted apparel, ladies dresses, candy, and shoes were produced.

Prominent businessmen of the late 1800s and early 1900s built houses in an area now known as the Center Avenue Historic District. Eight of the homes are over 100 years old, and many still reflect their original integrity. This area was placed in the National Register of Historic Places in 1993.

One of the first frame buildings to be erected in Jenny was a shed constructed by Joseph Beseau, who with Jules Posey operated a trading post there. The Posey Dining Hall, located in the 800 block of East Main Street, was erected in 1863 by Posey near the site where the trading post once stood. (Courtesy of MHS.)

The 1890s Parker Boarding House was located on 106 North Prospect Street. The proprietor was Nehemiah Parker, who came to Merrill in 1880, purchased land, and helped build many of the largest mills in the valley. He served as a sergeant in Company C, 41st Infantry in the Union army during the Civil War. He died in Merrill on January 20, 1904. (Courtesy of MHS.)

The first regularly organized fire department was established in 1887 with Julius Theilman as chief. The first East Side fire-engine house was erected in 1890; that same year, two horse-drawn hose carts were added. Below, a horse-drawn hook and ladder truck was added to the fleet of hose carts in 1892. A paid driver for this apparatus was employed in 1894. The two-story brick East Side engine house was built in 1917 and contained sleeping quarters for the chief and department members, as well as a billiard room. (Both courtesy of MHS.)

The new Lincoln County Jail was built in 1911 of cut stone and brick at a cost of $37,000 and included the sheriff's residence and office. Located at 1104 East First Street, across from the courthouse, it was demolished in 1980. (Photograph by Sam Leisman, courtesy of MHS.)

Members of the East Side Fire Department are shown here in 1913. From left to right, they are Chief Andrew Milspaugh, Mayor Joseph Emerich with Buster the mascot, Andrew Danielson, Adlor Talbot, and unidentified fire department personnel. This combination truck was the first motor fire truck in the Wisconsin River Valley. (Photograph by Sam Leisman, courtesy of MHS.)

Sigmund Heineman department store was located in the 1000 Block of East Main Street. Heineman came to the United States in 1871 and settled in Jenny in 1880. His small store soon became a leading business with the completion of the railroad. In 1892, he sold his store to David Livingston and was instrumental in organizing the National Bank of Merrill. Heineman was president of this bank and its successor, Citizens National Bank, until his death in 1913. He also was president and founder of Heineman Lumber Company. Heineman and his sons Harry and Edgar were true leaders in creating the successful community of Merrill. Below, Livingston's department store, seen around 1909, went on to become a mainstay in the Merrill community for many years. (Above, courtesy of MHS; below, TBSFL.)

The interior of Emerich and Staats department store is pictured here in the late 1890s. From left to right are Charles Thiel, Angus Bertrand, Edward Staats, Joseph Emerich, and Minnie Erdman. (Courtesy of TBSFL.)

In 1893, Joseph Emerich and Edward Staats acquired property from George Rothlisberg and established a staple and fancy grocery that also sold flour, feed, and hay. In 1919, the Emerich Mercantile Company was organized at 1504 West Main Street. The company dealt in dry goods, groceries, men's furnishings, boots, shoes, rubbers, flour, and feed and also conducted a large wholesale business furnishing lumber camps with supplies. (Courtesy of MHS.)

Lueck Blacksmith Shop, pictured here, was located at 1301 River Street and the corner of Park Street. This shop was the first equipped to shoe oxen. One of seven shops listed in the 1893 Merrill City Directory, it remained one of the oldest, changing hands several times, first to William Nienow and later to Walter Ristau. Seen from left to right are Donald Ristau, Frederick "Fritz" Pfingsten, and Walter Ristau. (Courtesy of MHS.)

The Frederick J. Runge Harness Shop, seen here about 1908, was located at 1313 East Main Street. Learning the shoemakers' trade from his father while growing up in Germany, Runge first opened up his own business in Oshkosh in 1873. Upon moving to Jenny in 1880, he resumed the business and added a harness shop in 1885. (Courtesy of MHS.)

Gottlieb Schroeder was born in July 1842 in Germany. In 1856, he came with his parents to the United States and settled on a farm in Dodge County, Wisconsin. There, he was employed in the farm fields for $1.50 per month. In 1883, he came to Merrill, where he erected a hotel called the German House at 1300 East Main Street on the corner of Park Street. (Courtesy of TBSFL.)

The Merrill Woodenware Company began making tubs in 1905 under the name of the English Manufacturing Company. The name of the business was changed in 1907, when local Joseph A. Emerich took over and gained a fine reputation for building lard and candy pails as well as toothpicks. In 1924, the company had a maximum daily production of 1,200 lard pails and 2,500 candy pails. The company ceased operations in the mid-1960s. (Courtesy of MHS.)

Around 1,600 sawmill workers went on strike for three weeks in August 1892, citing long workdays and little pay. While the sheriff and his forces were unable to cope with the strikers, no injuries occurred, and in the end the workers were successful at reducing their 12-hour workday to 10 hours. (Courtesy of TBSFL.)

Mill employees are pictured here in front of the T.B. Scott Lumber Mill in the late 1880s. In 1892, when the lumber industry was at its peak, eight mills were in operation in Merrill. That year, 150 million feet of lumber were cut. (Courtesy of TBSFL.)

Smith Brothers Central Manufacturing Company, producer of sash (framework of wood holding the panes of a window in the frame), doors, and blinds, is pictured here in the late 1800s. It was located west of Polk Street between First and Third Streets. (Courtesy of TBSFL.)

The Smith Brothers Central Manufacturing Company crew is pictured here in the late 1800s. (Courtesy of TBSFL.)

Emil Ruder (far left), who for some 12 years conducted the well-known George R. Ruder Brewing Company, was born November 29, 1859, in Stevens Point, Wisconsin. Ruder's father, who had already established a successful brewery in Wausau, accompanied Emil to Merrill. In 1886, Emil bought the brewery his father had built on the corner of River and Nast Streets. When Emil died unexpectedly in 1894, the brewery was purchased in 1897 by Ernest Leidiger. The Leidiger Brewing Company went on to produce beer for Merrill and the rest of Lincoln County for about 66 years. Merrill continues to honor its brewing history by holding the annual Lincoln Lager Barleyfest, which benefits local charities. It has been held each October since 2007, and it celebrates unique craft brews, many of which are created in Wisconsin and the Midwest. (Author's collection.)

Len Kaiser is pictured inside the liquor store that bears his name. The store, located in the 1000 block of East Main Street, later became the site of the McLellan Store. (Courtesy of MHS.)

Horse-drawn carts share the road with gas automobiles on the 1000 block of East Main Street in this early-1900s photograph. Len Kaiser's liquor store can be seen on the right. (Courtesy of MHS.)

Elbert Evert Howland (behind counter), along with Olaf Norland, purchased the Weiss Hardware Company in 1903. Jacob Amborn (leaning on counter), Henry Schield (far right), and two unidentified men pose at the 908 East Main Street location. Although relocating a couple of times afterwards, Howland's Hardware Store was a constant in the community for over 100 years. (Courtesy of MHS.)

These unidentified individuals are pictured in Baumans Bakery and Confectionery, located at 818 First Street. The bakery was one of the first in the city, changing hands and names several times over the years after Otto Bauman first opened its doors. Finally known as the Merrill Bakery, it gained a fine reputation for producing excellent quality Danish bakery goods. (Courtesy of MHS.)

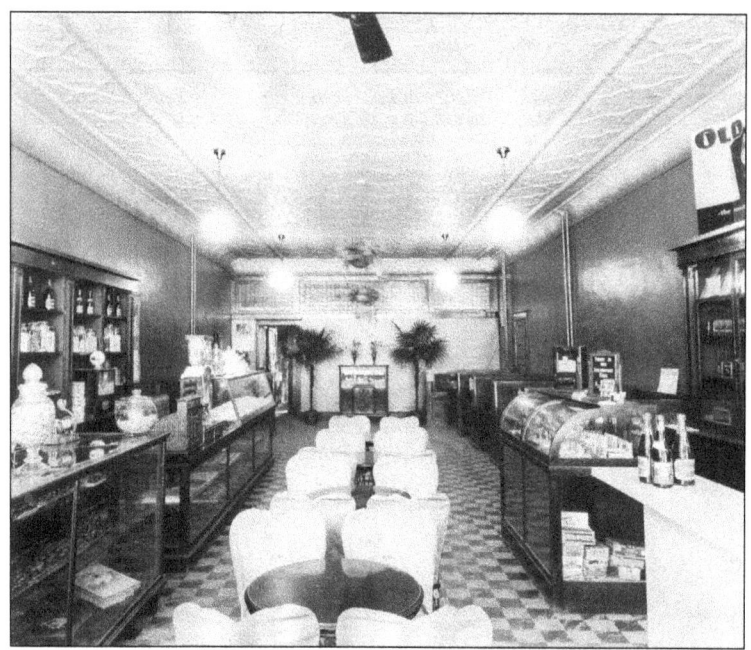

Seidel's candy store was a regular meeting spot for the younger generation. Charles F. Seidel and wife Mary manufactured all their own confections and ice cream. The store was located at 414 West Main Street and served the community from the early 1900s to the 1940s. (Courtesy of MHS.)

Stange-Wenzel Paint and Wallpaper store was located at 410 West Main Street on the West Side. Gustav Wenzel also established a hardware store in 1887, located at the corner of West Main and Genesee Streets. The store was a member of the Hall Hardware Company, which designated their stores as "Our Own Hardware." (Courtesy of TBSFL.)

Above, the Blair Cigar Factory was located on the 500 block of East Second Street. Hayden Blair (seated, front left) was proprietor of this establishment as well as the Mission Billiard Hall, seen below, at 113 Mill Street. The factory operated from the mid-1920s to 1942 and manufactured the Blair X-Tenso cigar, selling for 10¢, and the Blair Five-Cent Straight cigar, selling for 5¢. (Both courtesy of MHS.)

Leonard J. Kohlhoff and Charles A. Krueger opened their doors in 1911 on the same day that a flood swamped the area. While the load of souvenir carnations arrived too late to be useful, Kohlhoff Krueger and Co. persevered and, in 1922, moved a few doors east to 406-408 West Main Street. Selling only well-known and trademarked merchandise, the store gained a fine reputation. It survived early difficulties and served the community for more than 50 years, closing in the mid-1960s. (Above, courtesy of MHS; below, TBSFL.)

Crowds of shoppers filled a closed-off Main Street in 1977 for the popular summer event held since the 1960s. Crazy Day Sale, a chamber of commerce–sponsored event, included local arts and crafts, food stands, entertainment for all ages, and of course "crazy" low prices. (Courtesy of MHS.)

Sylvie's Style Shop was opened by Max Salmann on February 27, 1926. Named after his daughter Sylvia, it was located on the 1000 block of East Main Street. The shop maintained its own New York City office and bought goods directly from manufacturers. Sylvie's sold ladies coats, millinery, and hosiery and was known for reasonable prices, style, quality, and good taste. (Courtesy of MHS.)

The R.H. Trantow Hardware Company was founded in 1897 by Robert H. Trantow. Coal was added to the hardware line in the 1920s to accommodate demand. With the advent of natural gas, coal was eventually dropped, and lumber was added to the line. Today, Trantow Do-It Center can claim over a century of service to the Merrill community with the fourth generation of family ownership. (Courtesy of MHS.)

Julius Theilman learned the trade of butchering at age 14 and by age 18 had opened his own butcher shop in Grand Rapids, Wisconsin. In the spring of 1881, he moved to Merrill and opened a first-class butchering establishment and market, pictured here; he opened a second one in Tomahawk a short time later. (Courtesy of MHS.)

Cash Hardware Company, pictured here in 1915, was located at 422 Grand Avenue. William Voigt and William Schult were the proprietors. A dance hall was located on the second floor. (Courtesy of MHS.)

Rothlisberg's Grocery, located at 110 North Prospect Street, is pictured here in the mid-1930s. The building was previously occupied by Cash Hardware. From left to right are Wilma Fechtner, Clara Rothlisberg, Bernice Kobs, John Rothlisberg, and William Stuemke. (Courtesy of MHS.)

Wisconsin Valley Electric was located at 1029 East Main Street on the East Side. A series of eight 70-watt lightbulbs were installed in the T.B. Scott Lumber Co. mill in the late 1880s. The success of this system led to the extension of lighting to uptown stores and offices. (Courtesy of TBSFL.)

The Drew family has operated food stores serving the Merrill area since 1945. The family's first food store, an IGA, was located at 1501 East Main Street. In 1956, they moved to the 2400 block of East Main Street and about 32 years later to their present location of 3404 East Main Street, where they currently serve the East Side as Drew's Piggly Wiggly. (Courtesy of TBSFL.)

Located on Highway 51, now County Highway K, Club Modern, now Jillians Supper Club, has been a popular destination since the 1930s with ownership passing to the four families of Erwin Frisch, Elmer Raasch, Herbert and Julie Schulz, and Steven and Linda Blake over the years. (Courtesy of MHS.)

This is an aerial view of the Page Milk Company, located at 2200 Sturdevant Street. The business was in operation from 1925 to 1973 and manufactured evaporated milk and other dairy products. Page Milk distributed its products to the United States and allies worldwide during World War II. (Courtesy of MHS.)

The Gruett Drug Company was started in December 1914, when Albert Gruett, along with his wife and P. Amos Gruett, formed a corporation. First located in the Sixth Ward, a second store opened on the 400 block of East Main Street in the 1920s. They later added an appliance store. The name Gruett has been synonymous with Merrill commerce for nearly 100 years. (Both courtesy of TBSFL.)

Nelson's Rexall Drug Store and soda fountain was located first at 800 East First Street before moving to 807 East First Street. The drugstore was a popular gathering spot for refreshments and socializing from the 1960s to the 1980s. (Courtesy of MHS.)

In 1903, August Braun renovated the building at 416 Grand Avenue for the purpose of establishing a drug business for his son William, a pharmacist. It remained Braun's Drug Store until 1928, at which time it became Lussier's Drug Store, having been purchased by D.E. Lussier and his son Harold. (Courtesy of MHS.)

The Merrill City Post Office, located at 430 East Second Street, was built in 1915 and is the second-oldest post office in the state of Wisconsin. This building, with its classic revival architecture, was placed in the National Register of Historic Places in 2000. The photograph above shows the post office as it appeared in 1916. The building has since been updated to include handicap-accessible features, yet it still showcases a lobby that has been restored to its original design. Below, Eric Holstrom arrives back at the post office with a load of mail that he picked up from the train in 1929. (Both courtesy of MHS.)

The Badger Hotel and theater are pictured here in the mid-1940s. The establishment was built in 1904 in a flatiron design by architects Van Ryn and de Gelleke and located at West Main and Prospect Streets. A popular dining and entertainment center, it was gutted by fire in 1967 and subsequently razed. Pictured below is the elegant interior of the Badger Hotel in 1909. (Both courtesy of TBSFL.)

The Lincoln County Home and Hospital is pictured before the 1920 addition. Located on Highway 17, now County Highway G, the Lincoln County Home sat on 154 acres. The property, intending to be self-sustaining, featured vegetable gardens, orchards, and livestock consisting of close to 60 head of Holstein cattle, some 50 swine, and poultry. In addition to the large dairy barn, there was a large vegetable cellar, machinery barns, and poultry and swine barns, as well as garages. The Lincoln County Hospital was not strictly a charitable institution, although those unable to pay for hospital services were cared for without charge. (Above, courtesy of MHS; below, Ruth Pope Dreger.)

Originally Merrill's first hospital, the Merrill Hospital was built in 1882. It became the Ravn Clinic when purchased by Dr. Michael Ravn in 1900. This private institution contained 25 beds and was well equipped to meet the medical needs of the community. Dr. Ravn operated it until June 9, 1923, after which time it closed. Located at 712 East Second Street, the building was demolished in 1960. (Courtesy of MHS.)

Holy Cross Hospital was constructed in 1926 at a cost of $60,000 by the Sisters of Mercy of the Holy Cross. It was renamed Good Samaritan Health Center in 1987 when ownership changed. In the early 1920s, many local women joined the Holy Cross Sisters USA Province, which has been based in Merrill since the city fathers invited them in 1923. The sisters celebrated 100 years of service in the United States in 2012. (Author's collection.)

Unidentified visitors, or perhaps building occupants, pose in the early 1900s outside the residence of prominent lumberman and Merrill's first mayor, Thomas B. Scott. Construction began in 1884; however, Scott never had a chance to live in the home, as he died in October 1886 prior to completion. Scott's wife, Ann, took over ownership, but she died a year later in December 1887. Over the years, following the death of the Scotts, the mansion changed ownership several times. Finally, in 1923, it was given to the Sisters of Mercy of the Holy Cross by the City of Merrill. Although the sisters are no longer owners, the vacant mansion proudly sits atop Holy Cross Hill overlooking the city of Merrill. For some, believing that it remains cursed by the Indian chief who was angered at the loss of his daughter or haunted by previous occupants only adds to the folklore of this place. (Courtesy of MHS.)

Trolley cars of the Merrill Street Railway in the early to mid-1900s were four-wheel, double-ended cars using twin trolley poles in a two-wire system. (Courtesy of TBSFL.)

Merrill's trackless trolley was one of the first in the United States and the first in Wisconsin using electric power from overhead trolley wires. Utilizing solid rubber tires, it extended the street railway beyond the end of its traditional track rail system to the Sixth Ward. The trolley is pictured here with T.B. Scott Free Library in the background. (Photograph by Leon Downie, Courtesy of TBSFL.)

With trolley revenues declining and maintenance costs increasing, the trolley and street railway system was abandoned in November 1921 in favor of buses for public transportation. In this photograph, an unidentified rider prepares to board a bus in 1926. (Courtesy of TBSFL.)

On October 1, 1890, Congress authorized funding of $10,000 to test the "practicability" of delivering mail to small towns. Rural Free Delivery (RFD) was adopted by the United States in 1902. Rural mail carrier Alfred C. Podeweltz stands alongside his horse and delivery cart in the early 1920s. (Courtesy of TBSFL.)

Five
CITY OF PARKS

It was no accident that the city of Merrill was wrapped around the Wisconsin and Prairie Rivers. Settlers tapped the natural energy of the rivers to power the mills and then drew upon the abundant natural environment for recreation, relaxation, and sport. The Merrill community knew it had something special, and a parks commission was formed in 1903. Soon after, Riverside Park, located along the Wisconsin River, was established as Merrill's first community park. This was followed soon after by Stange Park, Stange Kitchennette Park, Cenotaph Park, Athletic Park, Streeter Square, Ott Park, Lion Park, Normal Park, Gebert Park, the Merrill Area Recreation Complex, and Prairie Trails Park. The area also features the 101,000-acre Lincoln County Forest, which is open to the public for a multitude of recreational uses. Council Grounds, one of Wisconsin's most renowned state parks, and a portion of the historic Ice Age Trail also call Merrill home. The Merrill area park and recreation system consists of approximately 854 total acres within the city; it includes trails (linear parks), the county fairgrounds, and eight public and private school facilities with another 920 acres of wildlife area just outside of the city. It is easy to see why Merrill can proudly wear the nickname "City of Parks."

August H. Stange, a prominent, successful lumberman and businessman in the city, played an important part in the history of Merrill's park system. At the age of 19, he took up employment at the HW Wright Lumber Company in Racine and soon after went into business for himself. In 1881, when Wright established a sawmill business in Merrill, Stange became superintendent and then in 1886 went into business for himself. It was his public-spirited enterprises, however, that have endeared him to the citizens of Merrill, two of which endure to this day: Cenotaph Park and Stange Park, with the latter consisting of two parks. The tract known as Stange Public Park, the earlier of the two, was built up from a swampy area and laid out in its present beauty as a result of Stange's gift of land to the city. His private park was given to the city in 1920 and became Stange Kitchenette Park. Cenotaph Park, with its massive marble memorial monument, was located across from Stange's residence on Ellis Court and formally given to the city in 1923 when it was unveiled. (Courtesy of MHS.)

Park visitors stroll past the Stange Park bandstand and Prairie River around 1910. (Courtesy of TBSFL.)

Pictured here is the Maypole dance, part of the May Day festivities held in Stange Park in May 1912. Bethlehem Lutheran Church, St. Francis Catholic School, and the former city waterworks can be seen in the background. (Photograph by Leon Downie, Courtesy of TBSFL.)

Two unidentified individuals enjoy the view from a footbridge in Stange Park. The park includes just over 11 acres and is located in the central portion of town along the Prairie River. Inside the park itself are beautifully landscaped areas, several walking bridges and self-guided trails, and at one time a public bandstand. Below, boaters enjoy a slow ride on the Prairie River through Stange Park in the mid-1900s. (Both courtesy of MHS.)

The natural beauty of the 11-acre Stange Park is evident here. Scenic walking bridges provide visitors the opportunity to bike or stroll through out the park. Below, the two-arch stone bridge, a sister to the three-arch bridge, spans the Prairie River in the park. (Above, author's collection; below, COM.)

Located on the west bank of the Prairie River in Stange Park, youngsters enjoy the swimming beach in the mid-1930s. This area was a popular recreation spot for youth through the 1950s. An outdoor, inground swimming and wading pool replaced the beach in August 1968. (Courtesy of MHS.)

This outdoor ice hockey rink got a lot of use in the 1940s when the Merrill Comets represented the city in puck battles. A.V. "Debs" Loud and Jack Loud were major movers in the formation of the Merrill team, which performed on the ice for several years. (Photograph by Phil Erickson, courtesy of COM.)

These federal Green Thumb workers—from left to right William Bartel, Albert Forster, Walter Maas, Art Brosowsky, Fred Pfingsten, and William Dupke—complete landscaping in Stange Park for the grand-opening celebration of the newly constructed inground pool. Below, swimmers enjoying nice weather pack the pool on the first day of operation in August 1968. The heated pool, aging and in need of repairs, was closed in 2012. (Both courtesy of COM.)

Riverside Park consists of 22 acres and is located in the southeast portion of the city along the Wisconsin River at the end of O'Day Street. Often used as a backdrop for professional photographs and weddings, it is perhaps one of the most scenic in the parks system. Because of its location on the Wisconsin River, visitors also enjoy fishing, boating, hiking, and wildlife observation. In the c. 1900 photograph below, the footbridge in the park is a popular spot with visitors. (Above, courtesy of COM; below, MHS.)

A crowd gathers for the Cenotaph Park dedication in August 1923. This beautiful monument was erected as a war memorial on a tract of land donated to the city by August H. Stange. It occupies the center of the smallest of Merrill's parks, located at the junction of Grand Avenue and Prospect Street. The monument was made by the Merrill Marble and Granite Works. (Courtesy of MHS.)

This log and field stone shelter is located in Council Grounds State Park. Situated along the Wisconsin River near the site of Native American encampments, Council Grounds State Park is a favorite for water enthusiasts. The 503-acre park offers many recreational opportunities, including wooded trails, a beach area, and an accessible fishing pier. A boat landing offers access to Lake Alexander, and there are several areas for shore fishing. (Author's collection.)

Athletic Park, a five-acre baseball field and historic landmark, began hosting amateur and semipro baseball games in 1925. The park is surrounded by an eight-foot granite wall, which was constructed during the Great Depression by the Works Progress Administration. One of the most scenic baseball fields in Wisconsin, Athletic Park is located on the corner of Sixth and Logan Streets. It features a lighted baseball field and restroom facilities. (Both courtesy of COM.)

Ground-breaking took place on April 17, 1994 for the Merrill Area Recreation Complex (MARC). Covering 96 acres, it includes softball/baseball and soccer fields, an outdoor/indoor ice rink, and other amenities. The MARC is located next to Council Grounds State Park, and the two are linked by a 2.5-mile multipurpose trail. Below is an aerial view of the MARC. (Both courtesy of COM.)

The Prairie River Dells Dam was constructed in 1906 by the Merrill Paper and Manufacturing Company to generate electricity for what became the Grandfather Falls Paper Company and, later, Ward Paper Company. It was demolished in the late 1990s. Since then, several lookouts have been constructed on the site, offering great views of the Prairie River. (Author's collection.)

Construction of the softball field in Ott Park is shown in this aerial view. The park, covering nine acres, includes a boat landing on the Wisconsin River, picnic areas, and a lighted softball field. Ott Park is located at the end of North Foster Street. (Courtesy of COM.)

A new gazebo was constructed in Normal Park in 2011 and dedicated to the Merrill City Band in appreciation for providing the community with a century of musical entertainment. The site of the first Lincoln County Courthouse and Normal School, it is a two-acre neighborhood park consisting of an outdoor ice rink with warming shelter. It is located on the corner of Sixth Street and Center Avenue, adjacent to the historic district. (Courtesy of COM.)

Merrill Memorial Forest Wildlife Area consists of a 920-acre wildlife habitat with walking trails throughout the park. Located off County Highway R, it is also a public hunting ground. The park also includes an 80-acre wetland area, recently named the Don Manthei Recreational and Wetland Area. (Courtesy of COM.)

Recently developed Prairie Trails Park contains 99 acres of pristine and natural parkland along a two-mile stretch of the Prairie River. Designated for canoeing, fishing, hiking, and wildlife observation and to promote physical wellness, the park contains 2.5 miles of multipurpose trails, a boardwalk, bridge, and a scenic overlook. Pictured above, a group of children visits the park to enjoy fishing in the Prairie River. In the photograph below are the shelter and fishing deck along a portion of the trail system. (Both courtesy of COM.)

Six
SPORTS AND LEISURE

Early local newspapers reported that settlers entertained themselves and others by holding dramatic productions and noted that by 1875 Merrill had two pianos. Despite working hard in the woods and sawmills, citizens found time for relaxation and entertainment. Parades were often organized to celebrate holidays and special events; an annual Labor Day parade is still held today. Horse racing, a popular event, was held at the fairgrounds in the late 1800s and was replaced by snowmobile racing at the same place in the 1970s. Merrill's first band was the Jenny Silver Cornet Band of 1875. A number of independent bands preceded the formation of a city band in 1911, which has provided the community with over a century of entertainment. The Badger Opera House held theater and stage productions before being destroyed by fire in 1967. The Cosmo Movie Theater started showing silent movies in the early 1900s. Surviving a fire in 1928, it was rebuilt and remains in operation today. Baseball leagues were established in the early 1900s, with community rivalries being settled on the diamond. Today, baseball continues to be a favorite summer activity.

With forests for a playground and a park system second to none, the pursuit of outdoor activities is endless. Parks offer trails for walking, hiking, biking, horseback riding, and snowmobiling and rivers and streams for fishing and boating. Ice drag races have been held annually since 1965 on the frozen waters of Lake Alexander in Council Grounds State Park. As fall gives way to winter, the sport of bird and game hunting draws hundreds of visitors with dreams of bagging a trophy. Recreation in the North Woods is more than just a vacation in the woods.

Cyclists from the local bicycle club pose with their two-wheelers in the late 1800s on the 900 block of East Main Street of the business district. (Courtesy of MHS.)

The Mission Billiard Hall, situated at 113 Mill Street, was operated by Hayden Blair. Blair was considered by locals to be a good "cueist." In 1923, he played Francis Hoppe, brother of the nationally known Willie Hoppe, in a pocket billiard match at a local parlor. Blair lost in what he considered a close match 125-101. (Courtesy of MHS.)

Above, unidentified children pose with an entry for the Grand Home Coming parade on July 4, 1913. Below, a group of young adults are dressed in costume as part of the same parade. While Merrill no longer hosts an Independence Day parade, Merrill's annual Labor Day parade is one of the largest in the area. The citywide celebration includes the parade through downtown Merrill, a classic car show sponsored by the Lions Club, and other activities held at the Lincoln County Fairgrounds. (Both photographs by Sam Leisman, courtesy of TBSFL.)

It is unusual perhaps to see elephants in Merrill, but the July 9, 1908, parade seen above was held in celebration of the arrival of the Gollmar Brothers All American Circus. The Gollmar brothers, born in Wisconsin and cousins to the Ringling brothers, started their own circus in 1891 and operated it until 1922, spending the winters in Baraboo, Wisconsin. Pictured below, chief of police Thomas Calder is seen (right foreground) walking along the circus parade route. (Both courtesy of TBSFL.)

A drill team, perhaps the Modern Woodmen, march down the East Side in an Independence Day parade held in 1896. The tracks of the streetcar system can be seen. (Courtesy of TBSFL.)

A crowd of spectators gathers in Stange Park in the 1920s to watch a game of baseball. Organized league baseball started in Merrill in the 1900s. (Courtesy of Tina Hipke.)

Members of the 1940s Merrill Golf Club enjoy an outing. These club members are, from left to right, Gus Stange, "Hans" Eggers, Jim Talbot, Bricky Stange, "Buck" Trantow, Jack Gilkey, and Elmer Eggers. Today, one can still enjoy the 18-hole golf course located at 1604 O'Day Street in the city. (Courtesy of MHS.)

A celebration for Merrill's 100th birthday kicked off with a centennial parade on July 3, 1947. The village of Jenny was settled in 1847, and the name officially changed to Merrill in 1881. The city was incorporated in 1883. (Courtesy of MHS.)

Whether for sport or sustenance, ice fishing was just as popular in the 1920s as it is today. The Wisconsin and Prairie Rivers provide ample fishing spots if the ice conditions are right. (Courtesy of MHS.)

Ice skaters are seen enjoying the frozen waters of the Prairie River in Stange Park in 1920. Today, several outdoor seasonal ice rinks, as well as an indoor rink located at the Merrill Area Community Center, continue to be very popular. (Courtesy of TBSFL.)

The Palace Roller Rink was located on the East Side of Merrill. Although the rink is no longer in operation, in-line, ice-, and roller-skating are still popular forms of recreation today. Below, a large group enjoys roller-skating inside the Palace Rink in the early 1900s. (Both courtesy of TBSFL.)

With net and fishing creel, Anna Callsen, is shown fishing at School Marm's Rock in the Prairie River, just north of Dudley, in the early 1900s. Dudley, a small, unincorporated community is located northeast of Merrill in the township of Russell (Courtesy of TBSFL.)

Several hunters, including William F. Krueger (sixth from right), pose with their trophies of black bear and deer in the New Wood area in 1934. There have been more than 160 regulated seasons of gun hunting in Wisconsin; the shortest on record, three days, occurred in 1937. Deer hunting contributes an estimated $1 billion annually to the state's economy. (Author's collection.)

The 1912 Merrill city baseball team competed with other city teams in the surrounding area. A very popular sport since the early 1900s, baseball continues to be enjoyed today by participants and spectators alike. (Photograph by Leon Downie; courtesy of MHS.)

The Merrill Rangers baseball team won semipro championships three consecutive years: 1951, 1952, and 1953. The team, first organized as the Merrill Merchants in the mid-1930s and renamed the Rangers in 1948, disbanded in 1961. (Courtesy of MHS.)

The Merrill city basketball team of the 1940s competed with other area community teams. These team members are, from left to right, (first row) Phil Sheil, Wally Gehrke, J. Behrens, Mike "Butch" Hudzinski, and Roger Zuelsdorff; (second row) Clyde "Oskie" Rampart, Jim Schmidt, Ray Isakson, John English, Jerome "Fromo" Rampart, and coach John Langlois; (third row) Norm "Elty" Kriewald, Jim Koblitz, Bob Akey, and Ray Bauman. (Courtesy of MHS.)

This 1931 Merrill city baseball team took the championship for the Wisconsin Valley League that year. (Courtesy of MHS.)

A group of young adults enjoys sledding at Schoolhouse Hill in Hamburg in 1912. Sledding is still a popular wintertime activity today. (Courtesy of MHS.)

The Fromm Foxes, a semiprofessional football team of the 1930s and early 1940s, was sponsored by the Fromm Brothers fur and ginseng operation. The team played the Green Bay Packers in Merrill on August 31, 1935; the Packers won 34-0. (Courtesy of MHS.)

Seven
READING, WRITING, AND RELIGION

In the past, one-room rural schools were so common that each community had one, including Lincoln County, which had more than 80 at one time. State consolidation regulations closed most of them by the 1960s. One such school, the Brickyard School, operated from 1905 until 1961. It was moved to the fairgrounds and currently is utilized as a museum showcasing the history of Lincoln County rural schools. The Lincoln County Normal School was established in the old courthouse in 1907 and served as a two-year college for training rural schoolteachers. It remained in operation for 60 years.

Religious services were held in homes or schools prior to the establishment of faith-based congregations. Methodists, German Lutherans, and Catholics all built and established churches early in the development of Merrill. Most of the churches in Merrill have historical architectural significance. The Holy Cross Sisters came to the United States in 1912 and, besides working in hospitals, established and taught in grade schools and colleges. Many local women joined the Holy Cross Sisters USA Province, which has been based in Merrill since city fathers invited them in 1923.

The Cain Creek log-sided school, pictured above in the 1890s with teachers and students, was located in the town of Pine River. The Doering School, seen below, was built in 1910 in the town of Schley. Many rural one-room schools served the Merrill community until the early 1960s, when rural school districts were consolidated with the city. Most school buildings were then either torn down, left empty, or sold to private individuals. (Both courtesy of MHS.)

Included in this portrait of the 1943 class at the Brickyard School are, from left to right, (first row) Ervin Schwartz, Emily Runge, and LeRoy Severt; (second row) Dorothy Wittwer, Laurice Severt, Yvonne Vorpagel, and Donna Klade; (third row) Marion Kanitz, Jean Dichroff, Jack Holl, Richard Klade, and Gordon Severt; (fourth row) Frederick Klade, Rosemary Boettcher, Mary Ann Klade, William Vorpagel, and David Donner; (fifth row) Evelyn Kanitz, teacher Myrtle Schumacher, and Ethel Adams. (Courtesy of MHS.)

This is the 1946 class at the Brickyard School. Pictured from bottom to top are (left row) Yvonne Vorpagel, Marion Kanitz, Mabel Moritz, and Richard Klade; (center row) William Klade, Donna Klade, John Zentner, Ralph Peterson, and teacher Doris Fruend; (right row) Donna Donner, Rowe Klade, Thomas Zimmerman, and Ralph Wittwer. (Courtesy of MHS.)

An unidentified teacher and her 19 students, along with a dog, pose in front of the town of Merrill's Barnes Creek School, pictured here in the early 1900s. (Courtesy of MHS.)

The Brickyard School was a house of learning for grades first through eighth from 1905 to 1961. It was so named due to its location near the Meyer and Boettcher Brickyards on Highway 64 east of Merrill. Now located at the Lincoln County Fairgrounds, it serves as a museum for Lincoln County rural schools. (Courtesy of MHS.)

Teacher Lucy Leisman (far right) and about 24 of her students stand near the corner of the Elm Grove School in October 1907. The school was located in the town of Scott. (Courtesy of MHS.)

Merrill High School Library Club students stand in front of the Marathon County Library Service Bookmobile in 1952. The Merrill Traveling Library Association, one of the first in the state, was formed in 1898, extending library services into the rural communities. (Courtesy of Marathon County Public Library.)

Pictured above is the Lincoln County Normal School class of 1937. From left to right are (first row) Edith Beatty, Myrtle Wendt, Anita Semling, Dorothy Harbath, and Annabelle Heller; (second row) Ruth Ann Krajewski, Alva Peterson, Vera Ecklund, Melva Umlauft, and Evelyn Early; (third row) Mae Price, Vivian Cumming, Ruth Pope, Phyllis Kellner, Monica Koehler, Evelyn Kellner, Mary Schneider, and Fern Schneider. Pictured at left are faculty members of the Lincoln County Normal School in 1937: from left to right are Lelah Gribble, Alice Gordon, and Jane Burke. (Both courtesy of Ruth Pope Dreger.)

Young members of the Christ United Methodist Church are pictured here in 1893. From left to right are (first row) George Sweet, Andrew B.J. Ladd, and Charles D. Dean; (second row) George G. Curtis, Leonard J. Bruce, Clair L. Stephens, and Frank Littlejohn. Below is the Christ United Methodist Church in 1906. Built in 1891 as Scott Memorial Methodist Church, it merged with Grace Methodist Church in 1964. The Methodist congregation is recognized as the first organized in the Merrill community. (Both courtesy of TBSFL.)

The original altar of St. Stephens United Church of Christ is pictured here before 1906. St. Stephens was organized in 1883 with 72 charter members. The first church building was dedicated in October 1884 and destroyed by fire in December 1919. The current church building was dedicated in September 1920. (Courtesy of TBSFL.)

St. Stephens United Church of Christ parishioners cross the Park Street Bridge over the Wisconsin River during a church picnic about 1909. The bridge, built in 1893, replaced a wooden one that was constructed in 1872 by Frank White. (Courtesy of TBSFL.)

The Estonian Lutheran Church is pictured here in 1975. Located near Gleason, this was the first church of its kind to be established in the United States. The church had 29 original members, and never having a full-time minister the handful of remaining members of the eroded congregation decided to board up the church in 1970. A small cemetery is located behind the church. (Courtesy of TBSFL.)

The interior of the Trinity Lutheran Church, located on State and Division Streets, is pictured here sometime between 1885 and 1907. (Courtesy of TBSFL.)

Pallbearers prepare to load a coffin onto a horse-drawn funeral coach during this early-1900s funeral procession. (Courtesy of TBSFL.)

The funeral of Henry W. Boyer was held in June 1907. Boyer served as city marshal and chief of police and fire for the City of Merrill in 1884 and 1886. Boyer also served for the Union in Company B and K of the 14th Wisconsin Infantry during the Civil War. (Courtesy of TBSFL.)

Eight

SEVEN WONDERS OF MERRILL

For centuries, people have been awestruck by the Seven Wonders of the World while not batting an eye at the wonders in their own backyard. Thus, the Merrill Historical Society began the Seven Wonders Project in early 2007 to encourage awareness and a greater appreciation of the many awe-inspiring treasures within the city of Merrill. The contest began in May of that year with an invitation to the public to propose nominees. Over 300 nominations were submitted, including sites and structures, as well as significant Merrill citizens, past and present. A committee of five community members selected 15 finalists from the submitted nominees. In mid-June, the public was invited to vote for its favorites from the following: City of Merrill parks, Bell Tower Residence, First Methodist Church, Church Mutual Insurance Company, Scott Mansion, T.B. Scott Free Library, First Street Bridge, Athletic Park, old city hall, Lincoln County Courthouse, Chips Hamburgers, Brickyard School Museum, Merrill City Band, Hans Von Kaltenborn, and Leonard Anson. The voting ended Labor Day, and the nominees with the largest number of votes had the distinct honor of becoming one of Merrill's seven wonders. The following pages contain the winners. With all that Merrill has to offer, the real winners are its citizens.

The first courthouse in Merrill was built in 1882 by David Finn. It served in that capacity until 1907, when it was converted to the Lincoln County Normal School for training teachers. Located on Sixth Street between Spruce Street and Center Avenue, it was demolished in 1968. The first Lincoln County Jail can be seen in the background. (Courtesy of MHS.)

In 1901, ground was broken for a new courthouse, shown here under construction. This highly stylized building was designed by prominent Milwaukee architects Henry Van Ryn and Gerrit de Gelleke. Visitors are still greeted by a majestic clock tower and inside by a stunning 50-foot-high rotunda, 5,000-square-foot mosaic flooring, and hand-painted murals rich with history. (Courtesy of MHS.)

The Lincoln County Courthouse was completed in 1903. A recent addition to the west side of the building was completed in 2011, along with interior restoration. It was placed in the National Register of Historic Places in 1978 and remains one of the most photographed buildings in the city of Merrill. (Courtesy of MHS.)

The Lincoln County boardroom inside the courthouse is seen here. All of the murals were originally hand painted and refurbished again by hand during a recently completed restoration project. (Courtesy of MHS.)

The Register of Deeds office inside the Lincoln County Courthouse is pictured here with staff during the early 1900s. (Courtesy of MHS.)

Herman R. Fehland is shown lying in state in the rotunda of the Lincoln County Courthouse in January 1907. To the left is Andrew Milspaugh, chief of the fire department, and to the right is Thomas Calder, chief of police. Fehland served as mayor of Merrill for one term in 1896 and in the Wisconsin Legislature from 1888 to 1890. Fehland was the first person to lie in state in the rotunda; Myron McCord, who died in 1908, was accorded the same honor. (Courtesy of MHS.)

The first city hall, built in 1889 and pictured here with a gazebo, is located on the triangular point formed at the junction of First, Second, and Scott Streets. Constructed for the newly formed city of Merrill, it was the hub of city government from 1899 until 1977. (Courtesy of TBSFL.)

City hall, seen here as it appears today, was placed in the National Register of Historic Places in 1978. Apartments were added inside the building during extensive renovations in 1993. (Photograph by Bob Gruling, courtesy of MHS.)

City hall was the original location for the T.B. Scott Free Library. The library moved into the building in March 1891. The city council, in need of a city hall to support the government activities of newly formed Merrill, decided at the time that both could be accommodated. (Courtesy of TBSFL.)

A new T.B. Scott Free Library was built near Stange Park in 1911. Pictured is the library in 1912. (Courtesy of TBSFL.)

The Merrill City Band, formed in 1911, has been in existence for just over 100 years and can lay claim to be one of the oldest bands in the state of Wisconsin. It was and continues to be a highlight in Merrill's social life and remains a constant on the city's summer entertainment schedule. A new gazebo was dedicated to the band in 2011, honoring its 100th anniversary. Many of the band's members are past or present Merrill High School band members. Above, the band gathers on August 27, 1952, and below, on August 3, 1930, it poses in front of the Lincoln County Courthouse. (Both courtesy of MHS.)

Thomas Blythe Scott, often referred to as the "father of Merrill," was born in Scotland on February 8, 1829. After accompanying his parents to New York as a young boy, he followed the westward movement in 1848, settling in Grand Rapids, Wisconsin. His main interest was in lumbering, as it was with so many others at that time. While a resident of Grand Rapids, he was a member of the state senate for five terms and introduced the bill in 1874 that created Lincoln County. In all his dealings, his reputation for honesty remained unquestioned. The early pioneer lumberman came to Merrill, then called Jenny, in 1878 with the intention of building a city. At various times, he owned a store, a bank, and a railroad. It was unfortunate for Merrill that he died a comparatively young man at the age of 57. One of the best things Scott did was make provisions in his will for a $10,000 fund to provide for a library in Merrill. Thus, in 1891, the T.B. Scott Free Library became one of the first public libraries in Wisconsin. (Courtesy of MHS.)

Nathalie Scribner served as the director for the T.B. Scott Free Library from 1922 until her death on January 18, 1948. In 1936, Scribner was instrumental in organizing the Wisconsin Valley Library Conference. Her efforts were an important first step in the eventual formation of the statewide library system in place today. (Courtesy of TBSFL.)

The T.B. Scott Free Library is located at 106 West First Street. Originally housed in the old city hall, it was one of the first 20 libraries in Wisconsin. The oldest part of the present building opened in 1911; later additions complement the Prairie-style architecture. It was twice named Library of the Year by the Wisconsin Library Association. The library was placed in the National Register of Historic Places in 1974. (Photograph by Bob Gruling, courtesy of MHS.)

Chip's Hamburgers is built over the footprint of the First Presbyterian Church, shown here in the early 1900s, located on Third Street at Center Avenue. (Courtesy of MHS.)

The Chip's building is designed in the distinctive architecture of the 1950s. Originally, it was part of a chain of drive-in restaurants but is one of only two remaining. It is the home of the Blue Jay Burger, real ice-cream milk shakes, and that unmistakable aroma at the corner of Center Avenue and Third Street. Regular patrons at the restaurant call themselves "Chippers." (Photograph by Bob Gruling, courtesy of MHS.)

The Brickyard School Museum was originally a one-room school, the Brickyard School, located in the town of Pine River. It operated as a rural school from 1905 to 1961. The Lincoln County Fair Board purchased the school building, desks, books, and school furnishings from the Pine River School District for $700. It was moved to the Lincoln County Fairgrounds in 1961. For 20 years, it was used by 4-H leaders, retired educators, and members of the Park City Garden Club for demonstrations and exhibits. On April 23, 1981, the board of directors of the Merrill Historical Society voted to accept responsibility to refurbish the interior of the school with photographs, albums, documents, and artifacts to interpret the history of one-room rural schools in Lincoln County. The museum serves as a reminder of the importance of these schools in providing education to the children of rural communities. (Photograph by Bob Gruling, courtesy of MHS.)

The First Street Bridge, spanning the Prairie River, was placed in the National Register of Historic Places in 1996. Built in 1904, it is the only three-arch bridge remaining in Wisconsin used for public travel. It is 130 feet long, and each arch features a decorative pattern of stones. Upon completion, the *Merrill Advocate* newspaper described it as "beautiful in symmetry and grace." It can be viewed from Stange Park and Stange Kitchenette Park. (Above, author's collection; below, photograph by Bob Gruling, courtesy of MHS.)

Nine
THE FAIR

In 1880, the land known as the fairgrounds was privately owned and being used for recreational purposes. A racetrack, as well as baseball diamonds, had been built there. The Agricultural, Mechanical, and Driving Association wanted full control, so in 1885 it bought the land for $700. Later that year, the Lincoln County Land Commission bought it for $4,500 with the idea of keeping it for recreation and as a place to hold fairs. The next year, it was given back to the association with the stipulation that the property must be kept public and the buildings and fences maintained in good repair. The Lincoln County Agricultural Society was formed in 1887, and the association was disbanded. Horse racing fell out of favor due to mismanagement and the element of betting and gambling, but after a few short years it was added again due to popular demand.

A new county fair was planned for 1888 with the emphasis on agricultural, livestock, and homemaking. Boys and Girls Club and 4-H club members began to participate in the 1930s, entering livestock, horsemanship, homemaking, and agricultural competitions for prizes and premium money (ribbons with incremental monetary attachments). Over the years, structures were added for use as exhibit halls, to hold livestock, and for fair office use; public restrooms were added in the early 1950s. The fair has continued to offer outstanding summer entertainment, carnival thrills, and exhibits annually since 1888. July 2013 will mark the 125th consecutive Lincoln County Fair.

Louis H. Gertson was a stunt aviator who drew fair-going crowds all over the Midwest in the early to mid-1900s. He attached lights to his plane and was known for his night flying stunts, twists, and loops. He also had a brief stint with the airmail service. While the work was steady, it was not enough for Gertson, and on November 30, 1918, he resigned, citing insufficient pay after just a few months on the job. Above, Gertson is in-flight at the Lincoln County Fair in 1913. Below, he stands next to his plane as inquisitive spectators gather. (Both photographs by Sam Leisman; above, courtesy of MHS; below, TBSFL.)

Crowds gather in front of the grandstand at the fairgrounds in the late 1890s. Horse racing was a popular event at that time, with grandstand tickets costing anywhere from 25¢ to 50¢, depending on the nature of the event. (Courtesy of TBSFL.)

The grandstand, shown here in 1988, was built in 1927 for $27,000. Entertainment changed in the 1930s from locals to nearly all professional groups. It had to be dismantled in early 2012 due to extensive damage caused by a high-wind event. (Courtesy of LCUWX.)

Prime locations for displays and demonstrations were located under the grandstand at the Lincoln County Fair. Above, a fast-milking demonstration attempts to improve on current milking techniques through a series of well-thought-out steps. Below, a local sewing-supply business, owned by Gerald Parmentier, has local seamstresses taking new machines for a test drive. (Both courtesy of MHS.)

Early fairs had only three amusement rides, a merry-go-round, a Ferris wheel, and the daring Whip. Today, carnival rides fill the "pike," or midway, from the grandstand to the stock pavilion. The Ferris wheel is still an integral part of the midway attractions at the fair. (Courtesy of MHS.)

A 4-H member is pictured with his canine entry for judging at the fair in 1988. Elaine Strasser judges while 4-H leader Shirley Lueck observes in the background. (Courtesy of LCUWX.)

The Stock Pavillion, pictured here in 1988, was built in 1927. The north wing of the pavilion was reserved for garden and flower exhibits. (Courtesy of LCUWX.)

Cows belonging to members of the Rock Fall Rascalls 4-H club relax in the barn. Members bring their 4-H project animals to the fair for judging. Fairgoers have an opportunity to wander the barns to view the prize-winning animals. (Courtesy of LCUWX.)

The first Lincoln County Fair was held in 1888 at what is now known as the fairgrounds. It was not until the 1920s that the 4-H program was introduced and became an integral part of the fair. Displays judged at the fair are still centered on the efforts of local youth and one of their projects from the past year, which can include animals both large and small. Above, a group of 4-H children gathers for the Holstein judging contest on July 25, 1938, held at the county farm. Below, children gather for cattle judging at the Lincoln County Fair in 1939. (Both courtesy of MHS.)

The Ferris wheel and other amusement rides are pictured here in 1988 at the Lincoln County Fair centennial celebration. (Courtesy of LCUWX.)

The concessions stands dotted along the midway attract fairgoers for the 1988 Lincoln County Fair centennial celebration. The taste of summer—cotton candy, hot dogs, frozen monkey tails, and chicken dinners—keeps fairgoers returning year after year. (Courtesy of LCUWX.)

Children enjoy one of the amusement rides at the 1988 Lincoln County Fair centennial celebration. (Courtesy of LCUWX.)

In the 1950s, as well as today, local groups come back annually to their concession stands along the midway. Staffed by members of the organization, it is a means of fundraising and a time to reacquaint themselves with local fairgoers. (Courtesy of LCUWX.)

The Lincoln County Fairgrounds is used for a variety of events outside of the annual fair. Pictured is a Memorial Day/Decoration Day celebration held in front of the grandstand in 1913. (Courtesy of TBSFL.)

The tractor pull, a popular event with spectators, was held in front of the grandstand. Big crowds gathered for this 1988 Lincoln County Fair centennial celebration event. (Courtesy of LCUWX.)

The demolition derby continues to be a very popular event, usually drawing a large number of spectators. Pictured here at the 1988 Lincoln County Fair centennial celebration, the event has each participant hoping to be the last car running. (Courtesy of LCUWX.)

Log rolling is a special event, added during the 1988 Lincoln County Fair centennial celebration, that pays homage to the lumberjacks of logging days gone by. (Courtesy of LCUWX.)

Hulda Vonderheid Barden, a 1921 graduate of the Lincoln County Normal School, taught in rural schools in the towns of Pine River and Schley. She spent most of her life working with the youth of Lincoln County. Barden served as board member and director of the Lincoln County 4-H Leaders Association from its beginning until the 1940s. She was instrumental in organizing and developing 4-H clubs throughout the county. In addition, she wrote and produced home talent plays and programs for the cultural development of 4-H clubs. Some of the programs were part of the grandstand entertainment during the annual fair. (Courtesy of LCUWX.)

Ten
MOTHER NATURE

Part of the beauty of living in an area with four seasons is that weather changes are welcomed and even expected. The unexpected climactic events, however, can have a social and economic impact on farmers, businesses, and residents. There have been floods as long as there have been rivers, and the city of Merrill has not been spared. The first such document of a great deluge was an overflowing of the Wisconsin River in June 1880. After a copious and long-continued rain, the river began to rise until it was higher than anyone remembered. As the mighty waters went rushing onward, property was destroyed, bridges were swept away, and the railroad suffered great damage. Two other such great floods occurred in 1912, with the first in July when a little over 11 inches of rain fell over 24 hours. Losses in Merrill were estimated at $210,000. The next occurred in September, and losses totaled a little over $12,000. Floods of varying degrees have occurred nearly every year in Merrill; the one that occurred on August 31, 1941, recorded the highest river level since 1884.

While flooding can have a devastating effect, nothing can change the landscape like a tornado. The city was severely tested when an EF3 tornado carved a path 22 miles long, and at point a quarter mile wide, on Sunday April 10, 2011. Winds were clocked at 140 miles per hour, and damages mounted to nearly $12 million. Miraculously, there was no loss of life. Mother Nature has challenged Merrill, but the spirit of community has persevered time and time again.

The rising waters of the Prairie River can be seen covering the running gear of a Merrill Street Railway trolley during one of two floods that occurred in 1912. The T.B. Scott Free Library can be seen in the background. (Photograph by Leon Downie, courtesy of TBSFL.)

Tracks of the Chicago, Milwaukee, & St. Paul Railroad were washed out in downtown Merrill by the Wisconsin River flood on July 24, 1912. (Photograph by Sam Leisman, courtesy of TBSFL.)

The 1912 Wisconsin River flood laps at the wheels of two old locomotives parked in downtown Merrill. (Photograph by Leon Downie, courtesy of TBSFL.)

Two different locomotives were parked at Merrill, possibly in an attempt to protect the tracks in the flood of July 24, 1912. (Photograph by Sam Leisman, courtesy of TBSFL.)

The devastating flood of July 24, 1912, shows West Third Street buildings under water. This photograph looks across Stange Park and the Prairie River towards Merrill High School. (Photograph by Sam Leisman, courtesy of TBSFL.)

This 1930s street scene on the East Side near Livingston's department store shows high snow banks. (Courtesy of TBSFL.)

The rising waters transformed a street into a river in the flood of late August 1941. A bicyclist and a boat full of citizens make their way through the high water. (Courtesy of TBSFL.)

A car makes its way past the bus station following the Wisconsin River flood of late August 1941. (Courtesy of TBSFL.)

The flood of August 31 to September 1, 1941, of the Wisconsin River was one of the most notable floods in north central Wisconsin. Caused by torrential rains from August 29 to August 31, three-day rainfall totals greater than seven inches were common, with one report of over 10 inches. Some dams and many highway and railroad bridges were destroyed. Above, the Wisconsin Public Service Dam has water over its banks. Below, a road grader and several vehicles attempt to traverse flooded streets in Merrill. (Both courtesy of MHS.)

Athletic Park is seen completely under water during a flood of the Prairie River in 1959. (Courtesy of COM.)

An EF3 tornado caused significant damage to the Merrill Memorial Forest Wildlife Area when it touched down on April 10, 2011. (Courtesy of COM.)

The Wisconsin River overflowed its banks into Riverside Park in 2003. (Courtesy of COM.)

The footbridge in Riverside Park is submerged by the Wisconsin River during a flood in 2003. (Courtesy of COM.)

This is a bird's-eye view of the Prairie River as it winds through Stange Park on a calm day in the early 1900s. Visible is the signature three-arch bridge and the sister two-arch span. The Badger Hotel sits overlooking the river; the T.B. Scott Free Library stands alone near the bandstand in the upper right. When not raging over its banks, the river provides a scenic charm to the city. (Courtesy of MHS.)

Once Merrill was established, the wonder of "what lies beyond" enticed homesteaders and business-minded individuals to continue traveling north. Pictured here in the late 1880s is the road from Jenny as it went north to Tomahawk. And so, it is here that we end where we began, because sometimes you have to look back in order to get a sense of where you are going. (Courtesy of McMillan Memorial Library.)

Visit us at
arcadiapublishing.com

www.ingramcontent.com/pod-product-compliance
Lightning Source LLC
Chambersburg PA
CBHW050655110426
42813CB00007B/2019